DATE DUE

Countries Around the World

Spain

Charlotte Guillain

Heinemann Library
Chicago, Illinois

www.capstonepub.com
Visit our website to find out more information about Heinemann-Raintree books.

To order:

☎ Phone 888-454-2279

⌨ Visit www.capstonepub.com to browse our catalog and order online.

Edited by Laura Knowles
Designed by Victoria Allen
Original illustrations © Capstone Global Library Ltd 2012
Illustrated by Oxford Designers and Illustrators
Picture research by Mica Brancic
Originated by Capstone Global Library
Printed and bound in China by CTPS

15 14 13 12 11
10 9 8 7 6 5 4 3 2 1

Library of Congress Cataloging-in-Publication Data
Guillain, Charlotte.
 Spain / Charlotte Guillain.
  p. cm.—(Countries around the world)
 Includes bibliographical references and index.
 ISBN 978-1-4329-6111-4 (hb)—ISBN 978-1-4329-6137-4
(pb) 1. Spain—Juvenile literature. I. Title.
DP17.G85 2012
946—dc22   2011015439

Acknowledgments
We would like to thank the following for permission to reproduce photographs: Alamy pp. **26** (© Felipe Rodriguez), **39** (© Chad Ehlers); Corbis pp. **9** (Sygma/© Julio Donoso), **11** (EFE/© Archivo Diaz Casariego), **12** (© Bettmann), **30** (© The Gallery Collection), **32** (© Jean-Pierre Lescourret); Getty Images p. **24** (Carlos Alvarez); Photolibrary pp. **22** (Bios/Michel Bureau), **27** (Age fotostock/Xavier Subias); Shutterstock pp. **5** (© Tupungato), **7** (© S. Borisov), **13** (© Martafr), **15** (© David Hughes), **17** (© K. Jakubowska), **19** (© I. Quintanilla), **21** (© Maroš Markovic), **25** (© Diego Cervo), **28** (© Criben), **29** (© Cinemafestival), **31** (© Olga Besnard), **33** (© Patty Orly), **34** (© Sergei Bachlakov), **35** (© Vinicius Tupinamba), **46** (© Christophe Testi).

Cover photograph of girls dressed in Andalucian costume, Jerez de la Frontera, Andalusia, Spain, reproduced with permission of Photolibrary/Steve Vidler.

We would like to thank Lawrence Saez for his invaluable help in the preparation of this book.

Every effort has been made to contact copyright holders of material reproduced in this book. Any omissions will be rectified in subsequent printings if notice is given to the publisher.

Disclaimer
All the Internet addresses (URLs) given in this book were valid at the time of going to press. However, due to the dynamic nature of the Internet, some addresses may have changed, or sites may have changed or ceased to exist since publication. While the author and publisher regret any inconvenience this may cause readers, no responsibility for any such changes can be accepted by either the author or the publisher.

Contents

Some words are printed in bold, **like this**. You can find out what they mean by looking in the glossary.

Introducing Spain

What do you know about Spain? Maybe you have seen pictures of Madrid or you are learning Spanish at school. When you think of Spain do you imagine beaches and bullfighting, or flamenco dancing and soccer? Have you ever eaten Spanish food or watched a Spanish film? There is so much that is famous about Spain, but there are also many things that are less well known to the rest of the world.

Country of contrasts

Spain is a country in southwest Europe with a colorful and varied history, stunning and diverse scenery, and a fascinating **culture**. It covers an area of 195,364 square miles (505,991 square kilometers), slightly more than twice the size of the state of Oregon. Spain's landscape includes sandy beaches, mountain ranges, and a large **plateau**. Many people visit Spain each year to relax by the sea or explore its cities.

Global influence

Throughout its history, Spain has been influenced by other cultures, and the Spanish language and customs have spread around the world. While Spain is no longer as powerful as it was in the past, Spanish food, films, and sports stars are still well known around the world.

How to say...

hello	*hola*	(o-LA)
how are you?	*¿qué tal?*	(ke-TAL)
no	*no*	(no)
yes	*sí*	(see)
please	*por favor*	(por fa-VOR)
thank you	*gracias*	(GRA-thyas)
you're welcome	*de nada*	(de NA-da)

The city of Barcelona is full of amazing buildings designed by the architect Antoni Gaudí.

History: Civilizations and Civil War

Fossils found in Spain tell us that early humans lived there 1.2 million years ago. **Prehistoric** cave paintings show animals that people would have hunted around 12,000 BCE.

Visiting civilizations

People from various Mediterranean **civilizations** later traded and **settled** in Spain. Phoenicians, from today's Lebanon, had settled in southern Spain by 800 BCE. They exchanged goods such as perfumes, oils, and jewelry for precious metals. Greek traders followed, bringing olive trees and grapes. By the 6th century BCE people from Carthage, in modern-day Tunisia, were **colonizing** southern Spain.

The settlers from Carthage were pushed out by the Romans, who arrived in Spain in 218 BCE and ruled for 600 years. The Romans introduced a good **infrastructure** and **Christianity**, but during the 400s CE a **tribe** called the Visigoths began taking land in the north. Then, in 711 CE, **Muslims** from North Africa invaded the south of the country.

Moorish Spain

The Muslim settlers were known as Moors. They ruled almost all of Spain and Portugal. Their territory was called Al-Andalus, with its capital in Córdoba. Muslim rule saw many great achievements in science and the arts, including farming developments and stunning **architecture**. The Arabic language also influenced the Spanish language. Christian rulers fought to regain land from the Moors for centuries, and by the mid-1200s only the southern Muslim kingdom of Granada remained.

The impressive Alhambra palace in Granada was built by Moorish rulers in the 1300s.

CALIPH ABD-AL-RAHMAN III

(891-961 CE)

Abd-al-Rahman III became the **emir** of Córdoba in 912 CE. He was an intelligent ruler, who defeated rebels and fought Christians from the north. Under his rule Moorish Spain became rich and powerful, and he became **caliph** in 929 CE. He had firm control of the country, and he even executed his own son for turning against him in 949 CE.

Ferdinand and Isabella

In 1469, two Spanish kingdoms were united when Isabella of Castile and Ferdinand of Aragon married. They were **heirs** to the thrones of their kingdoms, and their marriage unified Spain's most important Christian states. This united power drove the last of the Moors out of Spain.

Isabella was a strong **Catholic**, and under her rule Spanish **Jews** were persecuted. The Spanish Inquisition was set up to force Jews to **convert** to Christianity or be sent away from Spain if they refused. Muslims were also forced to convert. Although Ferdinand and Isabella ruled together, their kingdoms kept their own unique traditions and identities.

The New World

Ferdinand and Isabella paid explorers such as Christopher Columbus to find new trade routes. In 1492, Columbus arrived in the Bahamas and later reached the coast of South America. He was followed by the *conquistadors*, who traveled to this "New World" to claim land in Spain's name. Two notable *conquistadors* were Hernán Cortés, who defeated the Aztec Empire in Mexico, and Francisco Pizarro, who conquered the Incas of Peru. Spanish **colonies** were set up there and elsewhere in South and Central America, and gold, silver, and jewels were sent back to Spain. This was a golden age for Spain, but its wealth and power were gradually reduced by expensive foreign wars.

QUEEN ISABELLA OF CASTILE
(1451–1504)

Isabella was made heir to the throne of Castile as a teenager and became queen in 1474. Although united in marriage to Ferdinand of Aragon, she ruled Castile as a separate kingdom. She was determined to make Spain an entirely Christian country. She also wanted to spread Christianity in the New World, but felt strongly that the people there should be ruled fairly.

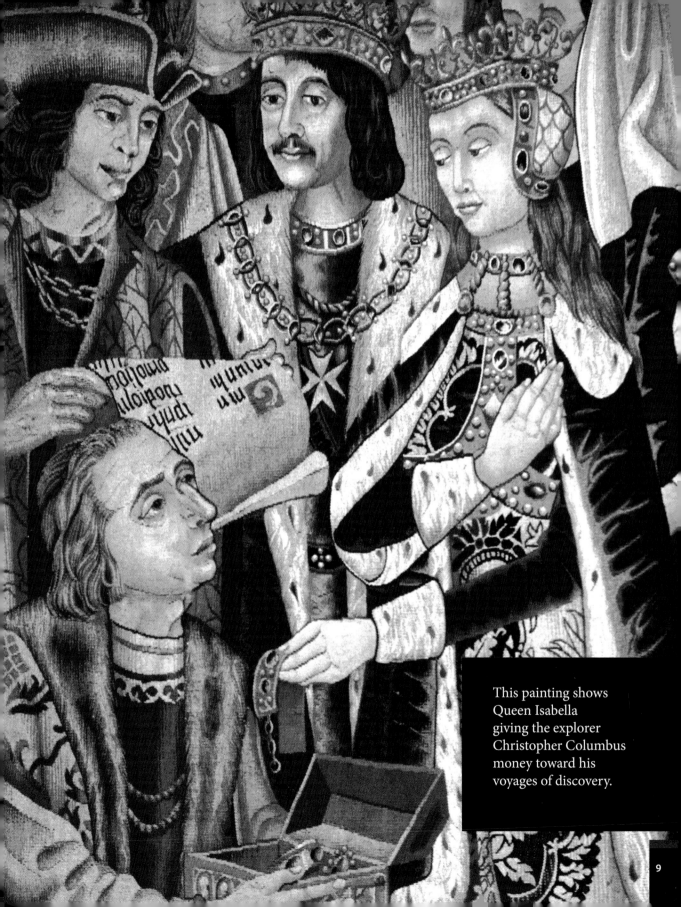

This painting shows Queen Isabella giving the explorer Christopher Columbus money toward his voyages of discovery.

French invasion

In 1700, Felipe V became king of Spain. During his reign, lands in Italy, Belgium, and Luxembourg were lost, but Spain was ruled centrally for the first time. The Spanish royal family had links with France and became involved in the wars of the French leader, Napoleon. Then Napoleon's army occupied Spain, starting the War of Independence (1808–1814). With the help of the British army, the French were eventually defeated, but chaos in Spain led to its American colonies demanding their **independence**. During the 1800s, more wars followed as members of the royal family fought each other for power.

Chaos and civil war

By the end of the 1800s, the Spanish government had become unstable. Workers and unemployed soldiers were unhappy about the unequal wealth of people in the country, and riots took place. This led to a **military coup** in 1923, resulting in General Miguel Primo de Rivera ruling Spain as a **dictatorship**.

By 1931 Spain was a **republic**, and regions such as Catalunya began to seek independence. The weak government seemed to have no control, and **anarchy** and **communism** had become popular. In 1936, the **nationalist** General Francisco Franco led military uprisings and seized the south and west of Spain, while the **republicans** held onto the north and east. The Spanish **Civil War** had begun and would continue until April 1939. During the war, as many as one million soldiers and civilians are thought to have died.

Daily life

Life for ordinary people during the Spanish Civil War was terrifying and violent. Both sides killed civilians in large numbers, and Franco's ally, Germany, bombed the towns of Guernica and Durango. Families struggled to find food, and some were divided by the opposing sides. After the war, the victorious nationalists killed thousands of republicans, and many others fled Spain.

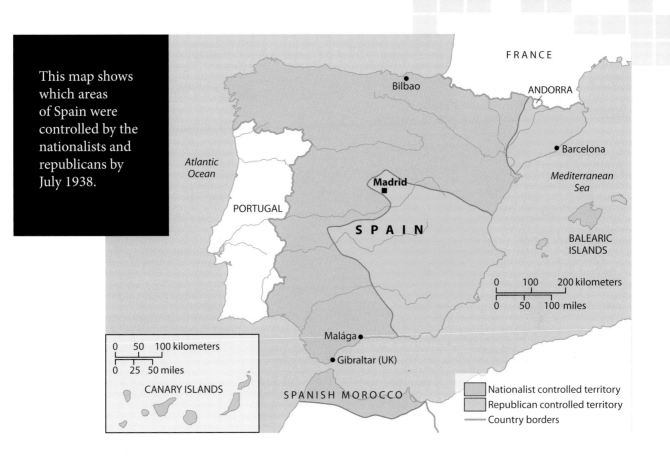

This map shows which areas of Spain were controlled by the nationalists and republicans by July 1938.

FRANCE

ANDORRA

Bilbao

Atlantic Ocean

• Barcelona

Mediterranean Sea

PORTUGAL

Madrid

S P A I N

BALEARIC ISLANDS

0   100   200 kilometers

0   50   100 miles

0   50   100 kilometers

0   25   50 miles

CANARY ISLANDS

Malága •

• Gibraltar (UK)

SPANISH MOROCCO

Nationalist controlled territory

Republican controlled territory

Country borders

These soldiers were fighting on the republican side at the start of the civil war.

Franco's Spain

General Franco ruled Spain for decades. He was the last **fascist** ruler left in Europe, isolating Spain from the rest of the world. The country's economy was underdeveloped until the 1950s, when the United States offered loans in return for military bases. After this, the economy developed quickly and life improved. However, Franco was a very strict and controlling ruler. Anyone who protested against his regime was imprisoned or shot.

A new government

In 1975, General Franco died, and King Juan Carlos became the next **head of state**. At first, very little changed. However, as more people protested against the government, King Juan Carlos saw the need for **reform** and made Adolfo Suárez prime minister. Suárez brought **democracy** to Spain, and this system of government has remained in place, despite another attempted military coup in 1981.

General Franco ruled Spain very harshly for more than 36 years.

Modern Spain

Spain has modernized quickly since the 1980s. It joined the **European Union (EU)** in 1986, and the Olympic Games were held in Barcelona in 1992. Tourism has expanded enormously, with huge building programs transforming coastal resorts.

However, Spain still has difficulties to overcome. Many people in the Basque region want to be separate from the rest of Spain. To try to make this happen, a Basque **terrorist** group called ETA has carried out bombing campaigns. The Spanish economy, which had been growing steadily, was hit hard by the global economic crisis in 2008. Since then, **unemployment** has increased and government debt has risen. Difficult times may lie ahead again for the Spanish people.

This stunning, giant steel sculpture of a fish was created for the Barcelona Olympics in 1992.

Regions and Resources:
From Alicante to Zaragoza

Spain has borders with Portugal, France, Gibraltar, and Andorra. Only a small stretch of water, the Strait of Gibraltar, separates the south of Spain from Morocco in Africa, and Spain still holds territory in Morocco at Ceuta and Melilla. The **peninsula** of Gibraltar itself is a British Overseas Territory, although Spain would like to recover this land. The Balearic Islands and Canary Islands are part of Spain but have some **autonomy**. Spain also has three small fortresses on the coast of Morocco.

This map of Spain shows the country's main physical features.

Bay of Biscay

N

FRANCE

Bilbao

ANDORRA

Pyrenees Mountains

River Ebro

River Duero

Barcelona

Atlantic
Ocean

Madrid

Menorca

PORTUGAL

River Tagus

Mallorca

S P A I N

River Guadiana

Valencia

Ibiza

Balearic Islands

Formentera

River Guadalquivir

Mar Menor

Seville

Mediterranean
Sea

Málaga

Gibraltar (UK)
Ceuta (Spanish)

Melilla
(Spanish)

ALGERIA

MOROCCO

0	100	200 kilometers
0	50	100 miles

Land height
above sea level:

	Over 6,550 feet
	Over 3,250 feet
	Over 1,650 feet
	Over 650 feet
	Below 650 feet
——	Country borders

Landscape and climate

Spain has a varied landscape, ranging from high **plateaus** to dry, desert-like regions in the south, beautiful beaches and islands, and several mountain ranges. The longest river in Spain is the Ebro, which flows for 565 miles (910 kilometers). The largest lake is Lake Sanabria. Around 27 percent of Spain's land is used for **arable farming**. Spain's main agricultural produce is grain, vegetables, olives, grapes, and citrus fruit.

Spain's climate is **temperate**, with hot summers and cold winters inland, while the winter months are cool around the Spanish coastline.

The Pyrenees mountain range lies along the border with France.

Spain's regions

Spain's 17 regions are famous for their individuality and fiercely proud **identity**. Each region has its own government and unique differences in language, **culture**, and food. Andalusia in the south is famous for its sunny beaches, old cities, and flamenco dancing. Aragón is home to the historic city of Zaragoza and the mountains of the Pyrenees. Castile-León in the northwest boasts beautiful cities such as Salamanca and Valladolid on the central plateau, and the mountains of the Sierra de Francia.

Catalonia and the Basque Country are both well known for their individuality. Many Spanish people living in these regions would like to separate from the rest of Spain.

This map shows the 17 regions that make up Spain.

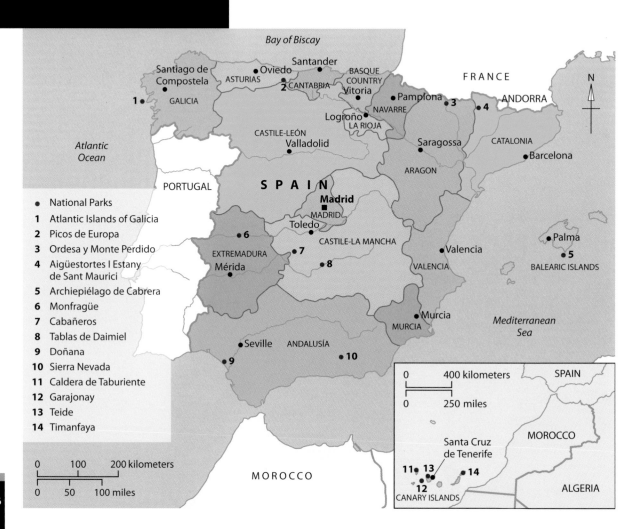

- National Parks
1 Atlantic Islands of Galicia
2 Picos de Europa
3 Ordesa y Monte Perdido
4 Aigüestortes I Estany de Sant Maurici
5 Archiepiélago de Cabrera
6 Monfragüe
7 Cabañeros
8 Tablas de Daimiel
9 Doñana
10 Sierra Nevada
11 Caldera de Taburiente
12 Garajonay
13 Teide
14 Timanfaya

The island of Mallorca is well known for its beautiful mountains, cliffs, and caves, as well as its sandy beaches.

Island life

The main Spanish islands are the Balearic and Canary Islands. Mallorca, Menorca, Ibiza, and Formentera make up the Balearic Islands, which are a popular vacation destination. The islanders speak Spanish and Catalan and enjoy mild winters and hot summers. The Canary Islands lie off the northwest coast of Africa. Tenerife is the largest island, which is home to Teide National Park. All the Canary Islands are volcanic, and a few active volcanoes remain.

Daily life

The regions of Spain have their own customs and festivals. Pamplona in Navarre is famous for a festival where bulls run through the streets. The town of Buñol celebrates *La Tomatina*, when thousands of people throw tomatoes at each other. In April, Seville celebrates a week-long festival with plenty of bullfighting. Catalonia remembers September 11 as the day it lost its **independence** from the rest of Spain.

The economy

Spain has struggled to recover from the economic damage and lack of development caused by years of war and isolation from the rest of the world. The late 20th century and early 21st century was a period of growth, but **recession** hit Spain in 2008, and it will take some time to recover. **Unemployment** is high among young people because it is expensive for employers to let long-term employees go. In addition, the construction industry has declined and house prices have fallen. Other countries in the EU may have to support Spain to prevent economic collapse.

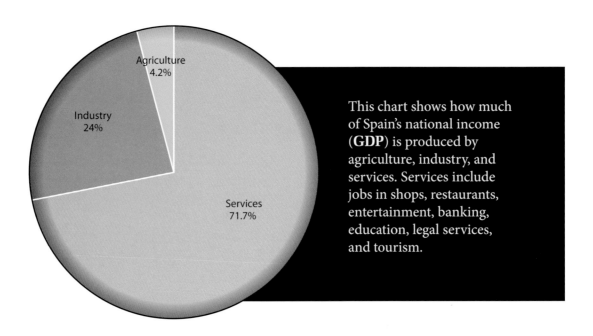

Agriculture 4.2%

Industry 24%

Services 71.7%

This chart shows how much of Spain's national income (**GDP**) is produced by agriculture, industry, and services. Services include jobs in shops, restaurants, entertainment, banking, education, legal services, and tourism.

Industry and natural resources

Spanish factories produce a range of goods. Some of the main industries include textiles and clothing production, food and drink production, metal production, chemicals, shipbuilding, cars, tools, clay, and medical supplies. Tourism is also a huge industry in Spain.

Some important **natural resources** found in Spain include coal, lignite (brown coal), copper, lead, zinc, uranium, tungsten, mercury, and other minerals. Fertile farmland is another important natural resource. Spain's rivers are used to generate **hydroelectric** power, and Spain is the world's fourth biggest producer of wind power. A solar energy power tower near Seville collects sunlight reflected by 624 large mirrors. By 2013, the tower is expected to provide energy for 180,000 homes in Seville.

The hot climate in the south of Spain makes it possible for solar energy to be collected and used to create electricity.

Wildlife: Protecting the Environment

There are ten national parks in mainland Spain, covering 473 square miles (1,226 square kilometers). The Doñana National Park is located in the Andalusia region and is one of Europe's largest wetlands. This park is made up of marshes and sand dunes and is home to many different species, such as flamingo, lynx, deer, and **migratory** birds. Visitor numbers are limited in order to reduce the impact on the environment.

Ordesa National Park covers 62 square miles (160 square kilometers) in the Pyrenees. **Glaciers** have carved out huge cliffs and valleys in the park, much of which can only be accessed on foot. Flowers here include orchids, edelweiss, and gentians.

The Timanfaya National Park is on the island of Lanzarote and covers 20 square miles (52 square kilometers). Volcanoes known as the Fire Mountains (*Montañas del Fuego*) can be found here.

Spanish wildlife

Some common animals in Spain include hedgehogs, rabbits, deer, wild boar, and ibex (a type of wild goat). Brown bears and European wolves still live in the wilder areas of the northeast. In mountainous areas chamois (a goat-like animal) and eagle owls can be found. Other birds include the Spanish imperial eagle, the buzzard, and the black vulture.

Spain's seas and rivers are home to many types of fish and shellfish. Common species include pilchard, swordfish, red mullet, mackerel, anchovy, and octopus. Dolphins and whales also live off the coast of southeast Spain.

This waterfall is in the beautiful Ordesa National Park.

How to say...

mink	*visón*	(bee-SON)
linx	*lince*	(LIN-tze)
whale	*ballena*	(ba-LLEH-nah)
hare	*liebre*	(LEE-eh-breh)
mouse	*ratón*	(rah-TON)
bat	*murciélago*	(moor-CIE-lah-goh)
seal	*foca*	(FO-kah)

Threatened species

The Iberian lynx is critically **endangered**. Hunting and destruction of its preferred **habitat** have reduced numbers dramatically, although **conservation** programs are fighting to increase the population and protect remaining habitats. The European mink is also threatened, with only a couple of hundred animals left in northwest Spain. Other vulnerable animals in Spain include the Barbary sheep, broom hare, garden dormouse, and many kinds of bat.

In the oceans around Spain, the blue whale, fin whale, northern right whale, and sei whale are all endangered. The Mediterranean monk seal is threatened by hunting and humans disturbing its habitat.

There are 985 threatened plant species in Spain. That is nearly 20 percent of all the country's plant species.

The Mediterranean monk seal is one of the most endangered mammals in the world.

The environment

Climate change threatens to impact Spain's environment, with fears of land turning to desert, particularly in the south. Spain already suffers from drought and forest fires during the summer. A controversial environmental issue is the vast area of greenhouses used for agriculture in Almeria. Many people think this damages the landscape, while others argue that increased productivity is good for the economy.

An EU law called *la Ley de Costas* is trying to protect the Spanish coastline by banning the construction of any buildings right on the seafront. One of the aims of this law is to keep the coast accessible to the public.

YOUNG PEOPLE

Thousands of schools in Spain have become eco-schools. This involves pupils helping to make their school more environmentally friendly. Some schools have added solar panels to their roofs to produce **sustainable** energy. Young Spanish people also take part in Young Reporters for the Environment. This involves writing reports and photographing environmental issues in their local area and sharing them with other young people around the world.

Infrastructure: Government, Health, and Education

A country's **infrastructure** is the set of systems and services that are needed for everyday life to run properly. The infrastructure includes power and water supplies, transportation and communication systems, schools, and hospitals. The Spanish government runs the country and makes sure everything works smoothly.

Spain has a type of government known as a parliamentary monarchy. The king or queen is the country's **head of state**. The government is led by a president, who is supported by three vice presidents. Each vice president is responsible for looking after a different aspect of the country, such as its economy and finance. These leaders are helped by a group of ministers chosen by the president. The Spanish people vote for representatives of different political parties in elections. Those who are elected join the National Assembly (parliament, or Congress) and the leader of the party with the most votes normally becomes president.

Since 1975 the king of Spain has been King Juan Carlos I. Many people think he is responsible for Spain's return to **democracy**. He has also competed in Olympic sailing races.

Health care

Each Spanish region is in charge of its own health care. Because of this, health care can differ from place to place, depending on where you live. However, Spain has a national health care system for all, which means all treatment, including basic dental care, is paid for by people's **taxes**. Most hospitals are modern and treatment is very good, although waiting times to see a doctor can be long. The World Health Organization (WHO) ranks Spain's health care system as the world's seventh best.

The **currency** in Spain is the euro. This currency, which is also used by many other members of the EU, replaced the Spanish peseta in 2002.

Education

Schools are also controlled by regional governments, so there are differences across the country. The government provides free education for all children, and school is **compulsory** for six- to sixteen-year-olds. Children can also attend preschool from the age of three. Children go to secondary school at the age of eleven for four compulsory years, and then they have three choices. If they want to go to college they can study to gain a qualification called the Spanish Baccalaureate. Alternatively they can choose to train to do a particular job, such as be a chef or a builder, or start work.

These Spanish teenagers are taking an exam at school.

YOUNG PEOPLE

A normal day in primary school starts at 9:00 a.m. and finishes at 2:00 p.m. In more and more Spanish families both parents work, so nearly all schools now have a breakfast club, which starts at 7:30 a.m. If children have lunch at school they stay until around 3:00 p.m. There are usually after-school activities from about 3:30 p.m. until 5:00 p.m., but parents have to pay for these. A uniform is optional in most schools.

Time out

School holidays vary from region to region, but all Spanish children have a long summer vacation from June until September. Parents who work often send their children to summer activity camps, or grandparents look after them. There are shorter holidays at Christmas and Easter. As well as closing on national holidays, schools also have holidays for special regional celebrations.

These families are waving off their children as they travel to a summer camp during the holidays.

An uncertain future

In 2010, Spain had the world's highest **unemployment** rate among 16- to 24-year-olds, at 40 percent. Many university graduates cannot find work and have to live with their parents while relying on **government benefits**. Those who do find jobs can often only get short-term work.

Culture: Flamenco, Fiesta, and Food

Spain's regions each have something unique and fascinating to offer, whether it be dance, **architecture**, food, or local customs.

Music and dance

One of Spain's most famous **classical** composers was Joaquín Rodrigo Vidre. Despite being blind, he was an accomplished pianist and composed beautiful guitar music. Spanish **opera** singers, such as Plácido Domingo and José Carreras, have become well known around the world.

Flamenco is a form of dance from Andalusia. A dancer is accompanied by a guitarist, singer, and hand clapper. The dancer beats out a rhythm with his or her heels, and castanets (a small percussion instrument) are sometimes used. Other regions have their own traditional dances and instruments, such as a type of bagpipe called *gaita* in Asturias and brass bands in Valencia.

This Spanish group is performing a flamenco dance, accompanied by music and clapping.

YOUNG PEOPLE

The Benicassim festival is held each July on the coast of Valencia. Tens of thousands of young people camp and listen to live music for four days. As well as international bands, there are huge dance tents where DJs play music all through the night.

Film

Spain has produced many actors who are famous at home and in Hollywood. These performers include Penelope Cruz, Antonio Banderas, and Javier Bardem. Spanish films are also popular in many countries, with directors such as Pedro Almodovar, Carlos Saura, Alejandro Amenábar, and Guillermo del Toro creating internationally-acclaimed movies.

Art

Diego de Velázquez painted portraits at the Spanish royal court during the 17th century. One of his best-known paintings is *Las Meninas*, which shows royal children and the artist himself at work. Francisco de Goya painted the horrors of war in the 19th century. During the 20th century, Salvador Dalí, Joan Miró, and Pablo Picasso painted modern, **abstract** art that was unlike any painting of the past.

Penelope Cruz has starred in both Spanish and Hollywood films.

Books

One of Spain's most celebrated writers is Miguel de Cervantes, who wrote the novel *Don Quixote* in the 17th century. In the 20th century, the poet and playwright Federico Garcia Lorca wrote during the **civil war**, until he was executed by supporters of Franco. Ana María Matute has written about life under Franco's rule, while Carlos Ruíz Zafón's novel *The Shadow of the Wind* was a bestseller around the world. Camilo Jose Cela won a Nobel Prize for Literature in 1989.

Don Quixote describes the adventures of a gentleman obsessed with knights and chivalry, who goes on his own imaginary quest. This is a painting inspired by a scene from the book.

Sports

Soccer (what the Spanish call football) is the most popular sport in Spain. The Spanish team won the World Cup in 2010, following victory at the 2008 European Championships. Fans follow their clubs in the soccer league passionately. Cycling is also a popular sport for professional and amateur cyclists. Spain is known for bullfighting, which used to be a large part of the country's **culture**. Today bullfighting is banned in Catalonia, and some other regions want to do the same.

Famous Spanish sportsmen include tennis star Rafael Nadal, Formula 1 driver Fernando Alonso, and the basketball player Pau Gasol. Successful sportswomen include synchronized swimmer Gemma Mengual and the mountaineer Edurne Pasabán.

Rafael Nadal has won each of the world's major tennis tournaments and an Olympic gold medal.

EDURNE PASABÁN   (BORN 1973)

Edurne Pasabán is one of the first female mountain climbers to reach the summit of all 14 mountains in the world that are higher than 26,250 feet (8,000 meters). The mountaineer from the Basque Country was presented with the Gold Medal for Sports Merit by the Spanish president in 2010.

Traditions and customs

Traditionally, Spanish people take a long lunch break in the middle of the day. This can be for two hours during hot summer months. Another tradition is to have a short nap (*siesta*) in the early afternoon. However, this custom is becoming less common, and people are working longer hours. Usually Spanish families eat their evening meal quite late. Family is still very important in Spain, and although people are starting to move away from their extended families for work, it is still usual for families to share childcare and leisure time.

Fiestas are a strong tradition in Spain. These festivals include *Fallas* in Valencia, *Los San Fermines* in Pamplona, and *La Feria de Abril* in Seville (shown here).

Food and drink

Each region of Spain has its own food specialties. Galicia in the northwest is famous for its hearty stews and pies. La Rioja is well known for its wines. Sausages are popular in Catalonia, and Valencia is known for its citrus fruits, almonds, and rice. Valencia is home to the famous Spanish rice dish *paella*. In Andalusia tomatoes, peppers, and seafood are featured in many dishes. All over Spain people eat *tapas*, a selection of small savory snacks eaten in cafes and bars. Typical *tapas* include olives, spicy potatoes (*patatas bravas*), Spanish omelette (*tortilla*), spicy sausage (*chorizo*), and prawns.

Tortilla de patatas

Tortilla is a common *tapas* snack. Ask an adult to help you make it.

Ingredients

- 1 onion
- 10 ounces potatoes (about 1 average-sized potato)
- 3 tablespoons olive oil
- 5 eggs
- salt and pepper

What to do

1. Peel and chop the onion.
2. Peel and slice the potatoes thinly.
3. Heat two tablespoons of oil in a frying pan and add the potatoes and onions. Turn the heat down, cover the pan, and cook for around 20 minutes.
4. Whisk the eggs in a bowl with a fork. Add salt and pepper.
5. Put the potatoes and onions into the bowl and mix with the eggs.
6. Heat one tablespoon of oil in the frying pan.
7. Pour the mixture back into the frying pan and cook over low heat.
8. Cook slowly for about 20 minutes, turning the omelette over halfway through.
9. Cut into wedges and serve hot or cold.

Spain Today

Spanish people are very proud of their nation. Although people still tend to identify with their region before their country, sporting events such as international soccer matches, Rafael Nadal's tennis matches, and motor racing bring the whole of Spain together. Parts of Spain are trying to preserve their own languages and traditions, and some still seek **independence**, but the country has remained unified since the end of the **civil war**.

Spanish soccer fans around the world celebrated Spain's win at the 2010 FIFA World Cup.

People come from all over the world to visit Spain's beautiful cities, such as the capital, Madrid.

People in many countries enjoy Spanish food and drink and learn the Spanish language. Spain remains a very popular tourist destination. From the sandy beaches to the mountains, and from ancient cities to tranquil hilltop villages, there is so much variety to explore in the beautiful landscape of Spain.

Spain faces difficult times ahead with an unstable economy and many people unable to find work. However, the Spanish people have lived through hard times before and can rely on their warmth and resilience to cope.

Fact File

Official name:	Kingdom of Spain
Official language:	Castillian Spanish (74% of population)
Other languages:	Catalan (17%), Galician (7%), Basque (2%)
Capital city:	Madrid
Bordering countries:	Portugal, Andorra, France, Gibraltar (UK)
Currency:	euro (€)
Type of government:	parliamentary monarchy
National symbol:	bull
Population:	46,754,800 (2011 estimate)
Life expectancy (total):	81.17 years
Life expectancy (men):	78.16 years
Life expectancy (women):	84.37 years
Religions:	94% Roman Catholic (Christian), 6% other
Area (total):	195,124 square miles (505,370 square kilometers)
Land area:	192,657 square miles (498,980 square kilometers)
Highest point:	Pico de Teide (Tenerife) on Canary Islands—12,198 feet (3,718 meters)
Lowest point:	Atlantic Ocean—0 feet/meters
Climate:	temperate; clear, hot summers in interior, more moderate and cloudy along coast; cloudy, cold winters in interior, partly cloudy and cool along coast

City	Jan	Feb	Mar	Apr	May	Jun	July	Aug	Sep	Oct	Nov	Dec
Barcelona	55	57	61	64	70	77	82	82	77	70	63	55
Madrid	48	52	59	66	72	81	88	90	77	64	55	48
Mallorca	57	59	63	66	72	79	84	84	81	73	64	59
Seville	59	64	70	75	81	90	97	100	90	79	68	61
Santander	54	54	57	59	63	68	72	73	70	64	59	54

This chart shows the average monthly temperature (in degrees Fahrenheit) of five Spanish cities.

Natural resources: coal, lignite, iron ore, copper, lead, zinc, uranium, tungsten, mercury, pyrites, magnesite, fluorspar, gypsum, sepiolite, kaolin, potash, hydropower, arable land

Major industries: textiles and clothing (including footwear), food and beverages, metals and metal manufactures, chemicals, shipbuilding, automobiles, machine tools, tourism, clay and refractory products, footwear, pharmaceuticals, medical equipment

Agricultural produce: grain, vegetables, olives, wine grapes, sugar beets, citrus, beef, pork, poultry, dairy products, fish

Imports: machinery and equipment, fuels, chemicals, semi-finished goods, foodstuffs, consumer goods, measuring and medical control instruments

Exports: machinery, motor vehicles, foodstuffs, pharmaceuticals, medicines, other consumer goods

Number of Internet users: 29,093,984 (62.6 percent of the population)

Famous Spanish people : Pablo Picasso (artist, 1881–1973)
Salvador Dalí (artist, 1904–1989)
Ana María Matute (writer, born 1926)
King Juan Carlos I (born 1938)
Antonio Banderas (actor, born 1960)
Carlos Ruíz Zafón (writer, born 1964)
Edurne Pasabán (mountaineer, born 1973)
Penelope Cruz (actor, born 1974)
Fernando Alonso (Formula 1 driver, born 1981)
Fernando Torres (soccer player, born 1984)
Rafael Nadal (tennis player, born 1986)

National holidays: January 1—New Year's Day
January 6—Epiphany
March/April—Good Friday and Easter Day
May 1—International Labour Day
August 15—Feast of the Assumption
October 12—National Day
November 1—All Saints Day
December 6—Constitution Day
December 8—Feast of the Immaculate Conception
December 25—Christmas Day

Spain's national anthem: The Royal March (*La marcha real*) is Spain's national anthem, but it has no official words. The music dates back to the 1700s. Words were written for the anthem in the late 1800s and again when Franco was ruler, but since 1978 it has been played without lyrics.

During the Corpus Christi religious festival in Spain, there is a tradition of parading giant mannequins through the streets.

Timeline

BCE means "before the common era." When this appears after a date it refers to the number of years before the Christian religion began. BCE dates are always counted backward.

CE means "common era." When this appears after a date, it refers to the time after the Christian religion began.

12,000 BCE	Early humans make cave paintings showing animals they hunted
800 BCE	Phoenicians **settle** in the south of Spain
600s BCE	Greek traders settle in Spain
218 BCE	Romans arrive in Spain
400s CE	Visigoths begin taking land in the north of Spain
711 CE	**Muslims** from North Africa invade the south of Spain
around 722 CE	Christians in the north start fighting the Moors in the south to reclaim land. This ongoing battle is called the *Reconquista*.
912 CE	Abd-al-Rahman III becomes the **emir** of Córdoba
1085	The Christian kingdom of Castile takes the Muslim city of Toledo
1249	Granada is the only remaining Muslim kingdom in Spain and Portugal
1469	Isabella of Castile marries Ferdinand of Aragon
1478	The Spanish Inquisition is set up
1492	Ferdinand and Isabella take Granada. Thousands of **Jews** are expelled from Spain. Christopher Columbus sails to the Bahamas.
1521	Hernán Cortés conquers the Aztec Empire
1533	Francisco Pizarro conquers the Inca Empire
1580	Spain rules Portugal for 60 years
1600	Spain controls Florida

1700	Felipe V becomes king of Spain
1713	Spain loses Gibraltar to Great Britain
1761	Spain gets involved in Napoleon of France's wars
1763	Spain loses Florida to Great Britain
1808	French occupation of Spain begins
1809	Spain's American **colonies** start to gain **independence**
1909	Violent riots in Barcelona
1923	General Miguel Primo de Rivera leads a **military coup** and rules as a dictator
1931	Spain becomes a **republic**
1936	General Franco leads **Nationalist** rebels against the **Republican** government and the Spanish **Civil War** begins
1939	Civil war ends and Franco becomes ruler of Spain
1955	Spain joins the United Nations
1959	The Basque **terrorist** group ETA is founded, seeking independence for the Basque Country
1960s	Spain starts to become popular as a tourist destination
1975	Franco dies and King Juan Carlos I becomes **head of state**
1981	An attempted military coup fails when it is not supported by the king
1982	Spain joins the North Atlantic Treaty Organization (NATO)
1986	Spain joins the **EU**
1992	The Olympic Games are held in Barcelona
2002	Spain starts to use the euro as its **currency**
2004	Islamic terrorists opposed to Spain's involvement in the Iraq War carry out bombings on trains in Madrid, killing 191 people
2008	Spain's economy begins to struggle

Glossary

abstract in art, not showing actual objects or people, but using shapes and color to communicate

ally person or country that is friendly and supports another

anarchy lack of order and government

arable farming growing of crops

architecture design and style of buildings

autonomy able to rule selves independently

caliph type of Muslim leader

Catholic relating to a branch of Christianity that is led by the Pope

Christianity religion based on the teachings of Jesus Christ

civilization society with a high level of culture, science, and government

civil war war between people of the same country

classical serious, artistic music, often played by an orchestra or piano

colonize settle in and control another country

colony place settled in and controlled by people from another country

communism social system where all people in a country share work and property

compulsory required or demanded

conquistador Spanish military leaders who conquered people in North and South America during the 15th and 16th centuries

conservation looking after something for the future

convert make someone change, for example, their religious beliefs

culture practices, traditions, and beliefs of a society

currency banknotes and coins accepted in exchange for goods and services

democracy government of a country by its own elected people

dictatorship type of government where the ruler has unlimited power

elect choose by voting

emir governor of a Muslim region or country

endangered threatened with extinction

European Union (EU) organization of European countries with shared political and economic aims. The EU formed from the EEC (European Economic Community) in 1993.

fascist person with extreme right-wing, nationalist beliefs

GDP Gross Domestic Product; the value of goods and services produced by a country within one year

glacier huge area of slowly moving ice

government benefit financial help given to people who need support, paid for by taxes

habitat environment where a plant or animal is found

head of state main public representative of a country, such as a queen or president

heir person who will inherit something, for example the throne of a country

hydroelectric relating to electricity produced by flowing water

identity characteristics by which a person or thing is known

independence situation where a country or region can rule itself

infrastructure organizations and facilities

Jew person who is a member of the Jewish race or religion

migratory animal or bird that travels from one part of the world to another

military coup takeover of government using force

Muslim person who follows the religion of Islam, based on the teachings of Muhammad

nationalist someone who wants his or her country to have its own government

Natural resource raw material found in nature

opera play set to music

peninsula piece of land almost completely surrounded by water

plateau large, flat area of high land

prehistoric having to do with the time before events were recorded

recession period of economic decline

reform make big changes to the way things work

republic country without a king or queen, usually with a single, elected leader

republican belonging to a republic or wanting your country to be a republic

settle move to an area and stay there

sustainable use of resources that does not damage the environment and will also be available in the future

tax money paid by people to the government

temperate type of climate that is cooler in winter and warmer in summer

terrorist person who uses violence and threat for political or religious reasons

tribe independent social group, historically often made up of primitive or nomadic people

unemployment situation where a person has no paid work

Find Out More

Books

Barker, Catherine. *Spain*. Washington, DC: National Geographic Children's
    Books, 2010.
Berendes, Mary. *Welcome to Spain*. North Mankato, MN: Child's World, 2008.
Marcelino, Pedro, and Slawko Waschuk. *Junior Jetsetters Guide to Lisbon*.
    Toronto: Junior Jetsetters Inc., 2010.
Rice, Simon. *Discover Spain*. New York: PowerKids Press, 2010.
Ryan, Sean. *Spain in Our World*. Mankato, MN: Smart Apple Media, 2010.
Sheen, Barbara. *Foods of Spain*. San Diego, CA: KidHaven Press, 2007.

DVDs

Christina Chang and Shilpa Mehta. *Globe Trekker: Spain*. Directed by Ian Cross.
    London: Pilot Productions, 2002.
José Andrés. *Made in Spain (1 & 2)*. Directed by Bruce Franchini and Dominik
    Ciardiello. Arlington, VA: PBS, 2008.
Rick Steves' Europe: Spain & Portugal 2000–2009. New York: Perseus, 2009.

Websites

en.uefa.com/memberassociations/association=esp/index.html
Visit this website to find out more about *La Liga*, Spanish soccer's (what
they call "football") first division.

www.bbc.co.uk/schools/primarylanguages/spanish
Visit this BBC website to start learning Spanish.

www.spain.info
Look at Spain's official tourist website for information about the regions,
foods, and history of Spain.

www.cia.gov/library/publications/the-world-factbook/geos/sp.html
The World Factbook is a publication of the Central Intelligence Agency
(CIA) of the United States. It provides information on the history, people,

government, economy, geography, communications, transportation, and military of Spain and over 250 other countries.

Places to visit

If you ever get the chance to go to Spain, here are some interesting places to visit:

The Alhambra Palace, Grenada

www.alhambra-patronato.es
Visit the beautiful buildings and gardens of this Moorish palace.

The Guggenheim Museum, Bilbao

www.guggenheim-bilbao.es/?idioma=en
This museum offers tours for families in English and many art activities for children.

Museo del Prado, Madrid

www.museodelprado.es/en
Visit this museum to join in with family activities and learn about art.

Parc Güell, Barcelona

www.parkguell.es/eng
These gardens above the city are decorated with colorful mosaics and were designed by the famous architect Antoni Gaudí. You could also visit the Sagrada Família church in Barcelona, which Gaudí also designed.

The Sierra Nevada

In winter you can learn to ski and snowboard, or enjoy sledding on the snowy slopes.

Topic Tools

You can use these topic tools for your school projects. Trace the map onto a sheet of paper, using the black outline to guide you.

The red and yellow colors on the Spanish flag come from the oldest Spanish kingdoms of Aragon, Castile, Leon, and Navarre. Copy the flag design and then color in your picture. Make sure you use the right colors!

N

Madrid

Index

Titles in the series

Afghanistan	978 1 4329 5195 5	Japan	978 1 4329 6102 2
Algeria	978 1 4329 6093 3	Latvia	978 1 4329 5211 2
Australia	978 1 4329 6094 0	Liberia	978 1 4329 6103 9
Brazil	978 1 4329 5196 2	Libya	978 1 4329 6104 6
Canada	978 1 4329 6095 7	Lithuania	978 1 4329 5212 9
Chile	978 1 4329 5197 9	Mexico	978 1 4329 5213 6
China	978 1 4329 6096 4	Morocco	978 1 4329 6105 3
Costa Rica	978 1 4329 5198 6	New Zealand	978 1 4329 6106 0
Cuba	978 1 4329 5199 3	North Korea	978 1 4329 6107 7
Czech Republic	978 1 4329 5200 6	Pakistan	978 1 4329 5214 3
Egypt	978 1 4329 6097 1	Philippines	978 1 4329 6108 4
England	978 1 4329 5201 3	Poland	978 1 4329 5215 0
Estonia	978 1 4329 5202 0	Portugal	978 1 4329 6109 1
France	978 1 4329 5203 7	Russia	978 1 4329 6110 7
Germany	978 1 4329 5204 4	Scotland	978 1 4329 5216 7
Greece	978 1 4329 6098 8	South Africa	978 1 4329 6112 1
Haiti	978 1 4329 5205 1	South Korea	978 1 4329 6113 8
Hungary	978 1 4329 5206 8	Spain	978 1 4329 6111 4
Iceland	978 1 4329 6099 5	Tunisia	978 1 4329 6114 5
India	978 1 4329 5207 5	United States of America	978 1 4329 6115 2
Iran	978 1 4329 5208 2	Vietnam	978 1 4329 6116 9
Iraq	978 1 4329 5209 9	Wales	978 1 4329 5217 4
Ireland	978 1 4329 6100 8	Yemen	978 1 4329 5218 1
Israel	978 1 4329 6101 5		
Italy	978 1 4329 5210 5		